Co.

MW01531730

ISBN-13: 9798676209957
ISBN-10: 1477123456

Cover design by: Rachel Marie
Library of Congress Control Number: 2018675309
Printed in the United States of America

Dedicated to Mrs. Lawrie, my eighth-grade history teacher who told me that if I published a book, she would be the first to buy it.

CONTENTS

Copyright	1
Dedication	3
simple daises	11
deep roses	37
lovely sunflowers	71
heavenly magnolias	105

a note from the author

thank you for buying this collection of my thoughts.
more importantly thank you, not for spending money but for spending time listening
to my heart and i hope your own.
these poems have now been bound together as a physical copy of my soul.
i'd like to be honest and give you a warning.
simple daises will be, simple.
deep roses contains topics like depression, suicide, and eating disorders. I beg of you, if you relate to any of those poems, seek help and make sure you read heavenly magnolias.
lovely sunflowers will be full of love, friends and growth.
heavenly magnolias are poems about God, his love and what he's done in my life.

you've stopped to smell the flowers, i hope you enjoy their perfume.

writing a poem

i can feel it
the flowers on my skin growing
i need to sit
the thoughts are flowing
words i want to say fall out through my pen in scribbles onto an
old receipt
i receive
"i receive," i call out loud
as if the wind could hear me
i want it to know i'm proud
to write down the words it gives to me
it's in my bones now
the flowers are everywhere
and somehow
it doesn't seem fair
the wind that is blowing
has knowledge to share
but i, the unlikely middleman, have been given the burden to
bear
it blows through my hair and into my mouth
these words these words i have to let them out
but i, the unlikely middleman, don't seem to have the ability
to get it out perfectly
i stumble over my thoughts and my pen seems confused
the wind carrying this poem
must feel so used
i let it in and told it i would write it
but i've failed
so in this heartbreak i sit

SIMPLE DAISES

be kind

being kind
is lifting
the half dead insect
from drowning in the pool
it's not a necessity
nobody will be hurt if you don't
but choices have a history
of changing the course of everything
you can leave the insect
leave your unsaid words hanging like a noose
but if you speak
you just might
save a life

forever and always

i dream of sitting with you
in coffee shops in new york
on beaches so hidden they are unknown
and in the living room of our home
i dream of holding your hand forever
saying vows and letting go never
they say it's silly
to dream so big so young
to deem *you*
all i've ever wanted
but i'll fantasize anyway
because it feels like we got it right
and with you
i want to go through life
they also say
when you know you know
and i know you
you're the rhythm to my line
and i beg of you
always be mine

my two cents

drink coffee and tea
and do both boldly
read books
take walks
learn to cook
journal
dance slow
sing loud
learn to let things go

bellis perennis

there's nothing common about a common daisy
or at least there shouldn't be
beautiful alone
beautiful in masses
press and laminate them
paint them on glasses
white or yellow
pink or purple
they look good bundled
especially in a vase from a lover
patches of them seem to say something
like sophistication or a bee sting
they scream spring
and look good with wedding rings
they deserve more than the same slang as marijuana
and to be plucked by girls wondering if the boy loves her or loves
her not
next time you see a daisy
please stop
no need to smell them
they're not overrated like roses
they have understated beauty
isn't that what we all wish to be
simple and unconcerned
discreet and pretty
now that you're stopped
you can learn from the daisy

stay or go

you are like reading a book
except back to front cover
and bottom to top of every page
it's absurd gibberish
but i can't stop my perusing
i can't stop trying to understand
you're confusing
and frustrating
you're interesting
and i can't decide
if i need to put you down
or learn to read
backwards and upside down

have a smile on your face
a thank you on your lips
a hug in your arms
and a joy in your hips

the right timing

i'm just waiting for the clock to light up gold
for the rusting
ticking
hand to shine like a miracle
light up my room with an obvious shimmer
an undeniable sign

and she waits for the alarm she never set
to ding
and ring
a vibration she will feel in her whole body

he drinks
and thinks
and glares at the wall
as the minute's flare shrivels out
and a new hour approaches
not yet the time
it never seems to be the time

i wait
and i begin to hate
the tick
and clicks
and hums of cars passing
my mind is busy
running and dreaming
but i'm waiting
hating and envying
the ones who hear their alarm

i used to dream of the future we'd have
glimpses flashed like lightning
but it never seemed as frightening
as it did
the day you weren't there

i crave inspiration
words that move my imagination
that middle of the night type of motion picture
the one in my mind that i wish could be clearer
i crave depth
books with knowledge and complexities
not best sellers written by celebrities
i want to wear clothes that fit my personality
not what the trends beg to see of me
i crave friendship
friends that stop by instead of texting
sending letters and reflecting
good conversation about real issues pressing
not cloned characters daydreaming
i crave ideas
nature and books and people and looks
things overlooked like hidden rivers and brooks
i want to see life and death
take adventures, enjoy rest
let life come to me as I chase after God
i want to be something better
than these frauds

i miss you

funny how denying ourselves the usual pleasures we indulge in
leads to a longing for said denied item like never before

homesick

i feel sick
with one click
i can be home
but it's only a trick
i'm 5,000 miles from your zone
and i'm not content with the phone
my stomach aches with pains of missing you
the ocean loses its majestic blue
because being far from home is hard
who knew
i want to rest with the ones i love
so i pray to God above
that he'll give this season a little shove
and help me get to you sooner
i have a fever due to the lack-of-hold
in the evenings i get commonly cold
with no arms around me in a fold
it's like i almost see you but it's through a blindfold
i'm homesick
feverish and sore as a brick
no medicine can cure it
i'm on land but i feel seasick
looking at the ocean and the distance between us
i'm so quick
to call you and discuss
what life will be like when we're together at last
i can't wait
to have my own bed
shampoo for only my head
and your loving hand
in mine as we break bread

i'm free

so nice of you to invite me in your passenger seat but i already have my own car

don't fall in love with her
oh please oh please
my heart can't watch you love another

easy as pie

mentally i never went through the elementary years of my life
i can't recall a time things were simple and i swam and
splashed in a pool of smooth thinking
i've always been superabundant in all my ways
excessive in expressing my emotions
only recently did i come to understand the damage this does to
my soul
the heft of obsessively worrying
makes my chest feel like it's concaving
and it makes me want to relinquish life
when i think of simplicity i think of pie
me being in a lil house on the prairie with a checkered apron
and a husband who loves me
beautiful children sucking the honey from wild honeysuckle
i wish life were as easy as pie
i think i can choose to make it that way
but simple and hard are antonyms and it's hard to re-wire the
tracks in my brain
de-clutter my mind
burn the fears
go back to calmer times
wipe my tears
and bake a pie

hello

i love yellow &
i think sunset colors are the best hues to ever be painted before
my eyes
i like to be tan just to prove i'm a beach bum through and
through
sushi is a remarkable thing and i will treasure each bite every
time i eat it
i like to be comfortable but i get sad when i don't feel pushed
out of my comfort zone
my style changes every week
i take lots of pictures and write about everyone i know
i laugh loud and embarrassingly often
i'm a little bit defensive
but if i love you my walls are a sheer curtain
being grateful is my favorite pastime &
i can't stand the idea of settling in one place at one job for the
rest of my life
but i'll do anything the Lord asks
speaking of God i went from death to life when i was 14 and i
will never go back
my signature sin is my addiction to coffee
my family means the world to me
not everyone loves how i imagine love could be
and it pains me to see helpless homeless
& anybody starving
i want to fix the world and that frustration sometimes makes
me angry at everything
which then makes me angrier because i can't fix the world
when i'm making it worse getting angry at it
movies are usually boring
but theatre is my favorite kind of art
the ukulele sounds incredible
& i'm a sucker for anything acoustic
i sing all day
and dance in the mirror
my daydreams sometimes feel like a high it hurts to come down

from
love scares me but for someone willing i will dive headfirst
i hope my heart and the Lord smile on me as i live my life be-
cause i fear time will pass like a butterfly
spiders scare me more than death
and my biggest hope in life is that everyone feels loved when
they spend time with me

there is stillness in coffee
after the cream and the brew make love
there is rest
and the warmth of fulfillment

the bookstore and my five senses

sight:
-two black and white cats
-one man walking around with a baseball cap
-a book in her lap
-and books scattered across the table
-your hazel eyes passing love notes to mine

smell:
-old books
-worn pages
-musty... but still somehow clean and refreshing

sound:
-our lips touching between the rows of love novels
-low whispers of strangers' conversations
-the purr of one of the kittens
-the girls silky voice reading 'moonlight'

taste:
-the thick air
-i can feel the old pages on my tongue like an old wooden spoon
my grandma might have
-your lips

touch:
-thin books
-thick books
-paperback books
-hard cover books
-pages lined with carefully chosen words, i close my eyes and
pretend i can feel them on my fingertips like they were written
in braille
-your fingers
-soft fur of the sleeping cat
-wooden shelves that hold the hearts of so many passionate
people beating in their novels

but you see me

i got so comfortable being by myself
i don't really know how to let people in
i got so used to pushing people away
in the name of finding myself
i don't really know how to be found

i can't decide
if living
through the lens of my dreams
is saving me
or killing me

passing by

were always staring at something

the tv if conversation gets awkward
a book if you're a student
your dinner plate when the person across from you feels dis-
tant

we stare at the ocean on vacation until it turns our brown eyes
blue
and we watch life happen like we're not living it too

if it took all my strength to love you
i'm not sure i would
you're unique
but i never could
i'm too weak
too hold onto something good
my heart has sprung a leak
and it's falling onto bear wood
it will just get moldy
as it probably should
you don't want me
i'm too messy
nothing in me is good

under over

i under feel
i over-compensate
i over think
i over analyze
i over-use words that should be special
i over complicate
i over dress
i under
and over trust

social media

the world is dying
from an overdose on stress
we're all playing comparison like its chess
but the end of the game doesn't have a winner
we all follow and have followers
so who's the real leader

the allowing

i'm allowing
myself to feel what i feel
allowing the bullets
to sink into my heart
i'm allowing
myself to feel
i'm conflicted
i'm a little lost
i'm sad
i'm a little heartbroken
and it's okay
i can take a couple hits
i have firm armor
so tonight i'll let them hit me
as i lay on the floor
i'm not able to stand strong

DEEP ROSES

like sand
my thoughts slip
from my hand
my grip
too weak to command
my mind too fragile
to control
the things i think
what i think makes me sad
and now i'm here
like sand
blown by the wind
an emotional whirlwind

how do i get out
how do i get out
of my head
if i can't
i can't even get out
of my bed

i can't *just* cry
it's like every tear
is a capsule of a year
the floor
my childish safe space
where i first found God's grace
but now i'm older
one cry can't turn into weeks of downfall
one bad thing can't send me spiraling
i just can't ever cry it seems
because the tears fall like a rain of rocks
threatening to crack the glass house i've built over these happy
years

oh there it goes
how pretty is my potential
a balloon once always with me
now floating up the endless ceiling
my dreams and qualities
that make me unique
have been placed inside and exchanged for love
oh how lovely
affirmation of others
to feel like i fit in everywhere i go
how empty at night to know
i'm never really sure of who i am
i can't get back what i released from my hand

arguing

drone on and ride us in circles
but one day donuts won't be fun
and you'll wonder where i've gone

i wish i could say insecurity
is the monster
that swallows you up
and spits you out
but it's really the demon
that captures you
tortures you
and digests you
keeps you locked
in the deepest parts
of its stomach
and no matter how much
you kick
scratch and scream
it's a demon
it doesn't feel a thing

my stomach twists in
like wallpaper inside me
splitting off the walls
it curves in
as if it needs to be closer to me
as if it needs comfort
i don't even want to feed it
i love the feeling
of something wanting me

breaking again

don't fall apart don't fall apart
i tell my weary heart
stay strong stay strong
my head in my hands
i feel myself giving in
to the world again
don't fall apart
you've got a good thing going
you've been improving
but i feel myself giving in
to the world again
don't fall apart
you just put yourself back together
but my weary heart
can't take this weather
my confidence is an umbrella
in a raging thunderstorm
doing nothing to protect me
from breaking again

my heart is like a cheap silver necklace
i wear around my neck every day
it's getting worn down
it is visibly rusted now

a deep depression episode

take my hand and guide it to my pen
tell me what to do next, i'm too weak to form a letter
teach me how to hold a conversation without getting lost in my
head
remind me how to shampoo my head
pull me up from bed
can you brush my teeth for me
can you feed me

oh no please don't yell at me
i know i was staring blankly into the distance again
but i forget how to stand sometimes can you walk me to the
bathroom
i need help
can you put on my clothes for me

i know i was supposed to be awake an hour ago
it's hard to face reality sometimes
what was that
can i move with urgency
what's urgent about anything
what's the point of anything
why should i be urgent
you should just be happy i'm doing anything at all

i cry every morning
because i hate myself
and i want to wear makeup to fix it
but i know i'll cry it off later
so i wear my face naked
then i cry later
because i think i'm ugly
but makeup is only temporary
when i'm alone i'm still stuck with me
so i cry every morning

can you force me to eat because i'm afraid i'll starve to death
no wait get that food away from me

i'm hungry
but i'm hungry all the time so when am i actually hungry
can you prepare every meal for me

can you clean my room there's dust in every corner
i know you told me to vacuum but i was too tired
i'm always too tired

i was invited lots of places this weekend
with people who care about me
but i ignored all their calls
and cried because i felt lonely

someone help me
can you teach me how to smile
can you wipe the tears from my face because my hands feel tied
down but i'm starting to drown

just as the white scars on my thigh finally started to fade
depression came back to me like a brick to the face
like a razor to my veins

it's hard to kill your self
because depression is ironic like that
it wants you dead
but more than that it wants you to suffer
i want to live or i want to die
but depression wants me to barely get by

boundaries

there's just something about you that makes me wither
and that's not what healthy trees do

i can't count on you

recovering is so hard
when the people close to you
don't believe you have a problem

shallow

deep in feelings
yet unaware of my thinking
surface level
craving anything
the desire for pleasure
gets my mind racing
i'm thriving yet dying
and praying and prying
post-depression is passion
and passion is pressure
pressure pushing people to push past their potential to possibly
something more powerful
but it's shallow
it seems like deep waters
but if i looked i could touch the sand
the keys to freedom are in my hand
i'm confused and lost and
my eyes are blind to the land
conversations are clueless
cues leave me closest
to carrying the corsets
that have kept me cropped in
stitched in the shallows
of my own depression

i hurt myself again
solely because i think i deserve it
i don't know when this idea came to my head
but it hasn't left yet
i don't know where along my path
i decided i was worthless
but this demon that began on my shoulder
has crawled through the cracks
and made its way into my heart
i'm getting weaker as i get older
like a slow possession
my sadness consumes me
the dark side of my personality
overshadowing any light
i'm dying inside
and i keep hurting myself
i keep crying at night

i climb up the hill
i begin the trek
i've almost reached the top
then i slip
i fall right back in
like i never left

eating disorder's loving arms
are always open

lonely complex

how do i always end up alone
in crowds
or with my friends
in the shower
or with my mother
lonely as always nonetheless

desperate

i sit outside
and let my body freeze
because i read once
shivering burns calories

i've been sad

i was sure i was over this
but i'm once again starting to feel hopeless
i wish i couldn't relate to my old poetry but it sings to my heart's
melody

you said it felt like the weight of a car on your shoulders
you carry your regret and shame
on your back like it's a part of you
like the truck dragging behind you is something you were born
with
i see the sadness in those eyes
i hear the regret in your voice
when it goes from confident to ashamed
i feel your unease
your lack of self-understanding
in your touch
shaky hands glide across my skin
you don't know who you are do you
i wish you'd take the time to learn
to feel your own skin and kiss the places you once hated
tell the parts of you that you used to curse how beautiful they
are
heal
untie your cables and ropes
love yourself
release the truck
let it crash
and become yourself again

why would they
why would they
i cry to the shadows
they don't stay
they don't stay
i never wanted them

who am i to be sad
who am i
a mist of a personality
a burn-it-down fiery gasoline mist
just a daze
just a daze
one more day
one more day
until i'm aged and none of my self-loathing mattered anyway

i'm not better
i don't know what i expected
i want to die
and they all keep telling me
to fight
but ****
what am i fighting for

thoughts after a purge

my knees are bruised
my fingers are used
my throat is sore
and i wish i didn't have to eat anymore

ode to my depressed self

here we go
today, just today
you're going to pick yourself up
get out of bed, put on some makeup
you know you want too
put on clothes that aren't double xl
don't kill any bugs, be kind today
smile big
right now in the mirror, do it
why not go all the way, point out some things you like about
yourself
physical, or about your inner self
take a deep breath
today, just today
you are going to walk with your head held high
stop worrying about the size of your thighs
and you're going to enjoy these moments
you will never have them again
hug at least 5 people
today, just today
get some fresh air i don't care what the weather is like
we don't live in excuses
we don't live in our bed
you and me,
meaning me and me,
we live in the real world
read your bible
one chapter maybe just a psalm
pray and thank God for who He is
He doesn't change like you do
don't you forget that
today, just today
i want you to eat well
no bingeing as a coping skill
no starving as a way to hurt yourself
today you CAN stomp on those negative thoughts

i know you feel out of control
you don't always have to have it
let life not make sense
even if you just let yourself be free today, that's okay, just be free
for today
hey, maybe you'll like peace
meditate for at least 10 minutes
and remember that this isn't a perfect plan
you have flaws
you are human
you are not perfect
therefore no plan could ever work perfectly
but let me tell you what this is
this is today
this is your life
you get to choose and you will choose to make it what you want
not what the depression wants
depressed self
i'm talking to you
get up
wash your hair
eat a salad
don't care
pray like tomorrow you die
because tomorrow you might
and you don't want to waste your life
today, just today
read this poem and put it into practice
eventually
you'll do it every day

why can't i do it
i try to
but it feels impossible
i wish i could do it
i feel a desire within me to do it
but it stops me from it
it has control over me
or at least it sure feels like it
why can't i do it
i want it
i want a lot
and i know deep down that within me
is much more than i think is within me
but i just can't do it
i can't
i can't
i can't do it

depression wants me to disappear
but you want me here
depression sucks me into the dark
but i want to stop falling apart
depression tells me i'll never amount to anything
but i'm fighting to believe that i can be something

suicide sugar

i toy with the idea of suicide like hard candy
tossing it back and forth in my mouth letting its weight rest on
my tongue
"it's always an option," slides down my throat in sugar coated
saliva
though i know how selfish it is
and i know the stories of people who've almost died and i've
read that they are so happy they didn't
i've almost died
but sometimes i still envy the people who choked on the flavor-
less treat we all savor
they did what all of us want
and i can't buy into the idea that after you snap out of it and get
your life back
all the reasons you attempted in the first place
get replaced with the overwhelming urge to see the good in life
it just doesn't happen
or at least it doesn't last long enough to stop you from craving
candy again

i've written many poems about doing it all wrong but
    here's another one

i say the opposite of what i should
wear what isn't appropriate
keep people who i should shut out and push out the good ones
the ones who want to see me happy
it's ironic enough
my life
i could publish these words and die
perhaps leaving behind something intriguing
a good read with a sad about the author back cover
what do i do when the remedies turn deadly &
die out
they fade like the color in my lips
like the blue in my blood when the oxygen hits
my happy thoughts hold a kitchen knife
going to war against the army of darkness in my head with bun-
kers full of weapons of mass destruction
they tell me it gets better but what else would they say
the story of the sad children who grew up to be even more sad
isn't fitting for a poster in the psych ward
doctors can't look me in the eyes and tell me the truth
some days i'm ready to defy the odds
other days i do everything wrong

emotional abuse

she lets the sun scorch her soft skin
instead of taking the dive into the ocean
he's told her about the sharks down there
and she decided this pain is better than taking the treacherous
swim
so she stays on the island that is familiar
and never goes to the water

contemplating the aftermath

how shocked they would be
if i were to leave permanently
i wonder if God would let me see them from wherever he puts
the hasty
& angsty souls

they'd probably act like they had no idea
and i guess it was easier to live believing they didn't know
to convince themselves i never meant it when i said
this time i'll do it

LOVELY
SUNFLOWERS

your soul
it's beautiful
i want to touch it
i bet it's made of gold

progress

me then
would've listened to her tell me i'm ugly
and spiral out of control that evening
letting the words brand me
me now
would look into her hurting brown eyes
and recognize
the beauty inside her surpasses the lack of self-worth she holds
and i would tell her that
i wouldn't fold
she would know she's beautiful
and i would know the same

tough love

i don't wish to increase your pain
i just want you to be joyful again

gift

i gave you my heart that night
you were looking up at the sky
the stars served as a buffer
since my lack of words made my heart suffer
your arm around me served as a transfusion
my love
flowing to you

when you stare
don't undress me with your eyes
write me
write about how you like what you see
and what you hope someday to behold
i am more than shedded layers
so much more beautiful than simply what you are looking at
so read me when you stare
and write me if you dare

love

i think i want to tell you i love you
it feels too powerful
i've drowned in it before
got so deep i could no longer see the reasons i dove
i don't want it to happen again
is love an action
an emotion
is it head or heart driven
i guess it doesn't matter
i feel both for you
i want to learn about you
show love in action
through poems display emotion
i know
i can't tell you i love you
we're only friends
but something broken within me
will only mend
with honest and heart felt confession
i love your eyes
your smile
i love your laugh
your big heart
i want to tell you i love you

haiku to your heart

tell me what you love
i will chase it down for you
i want you happy

happiness looks good on you
let me kiss your frown away love

firey one

she's a blaze
walking around leaving a haze
healing and loving
being like Jesus until his coming
she walks with confidence
not arrogance
and when she laughs
she gives life to everyone who hears
fighting for the kingdom in a sapphire dress
leaving footprints of holiness
everywhere she goes
God is the only one who knows
what darkness this fire will light up
what corrupt fields she will burn down
and what mark she'll leave here on this ground
she's chosen
she's an encourager
fully loved by those around her
God's firey one
bringing flames in the form of love
to everyone

to the man i will love one day

my love for you is the right kind of love
and yours
equally right
fits in my palm like a treasure only i can see
like my eyes have a black light and your devotion is neon white
i fell for you slowly
and then suddenly
i woke up and i couldn't live without you
this is how i knew i needed you

they say that's the best way to fall and i found that to be true

i decided to love you
with all my love not already devoted to the Lord
i didn't decide this because of your beautiful eyes
or your lips that gave me the most tender kiss
i gave you all of me because you also gifted me what you had left
after
being fully enveloped in the Lord's love

relationships and i have a history
similar to skid-dish children and halloween

but you
the man i will love someday
i imagine you will make love feel safe again

personal blessings

it's so special
to keep a moment
like a vase of sunflowers
on a shelf only you can reach

for a friend

a rose
a diamond
cherished and lovely
your eyes make the Father happy
a tulip
a sweet cherry
your smile melts God's heart slowly
you're wonderful
and built perfectly
lovely from your head to your toes
he wants you to know
your beauty radiates
and he loves every inch of your face
you are a woman of grace
and elegance flows through your bones

like the tallest flower in a garden
you bloom and everyone stares
you release a perfume
into the morning air
and you release goodness
to everyone in your presence

this is how He created your life to be
so trust in Him
trust in what you cannot see

christmas

the excitement of knowing his eyes are fond of me makes me
heart feel like a christmas tree
in my mind every year i can't seem to enjoy what's around me
i'm thinking so constantly
about someone who i wish were here
i have yet to meet him and he has yet to win my heart
but i look forward to that special time of year when he finally
starts

future marriage

the tenderness that comes with giving is tenacious
giving your heart to another person is the most daring adven-
ture one can go on
they say you always get to know your spouse and if you acknow-
ledge this as true
then you
accept a promise and a ring
in exchange for everything
love in all its complexity is certainly never boring
what a humbling experience i'm sure it will be
to trust someone i don't fully know
enough to give them all i own

the pursuit

persistence is the most attractive quality in a man
all women just want to love themselves
so when a man chases after us
it opens the depths of our hearts to the fact that we are love-
able and worth a fight
when men make us love us
that's when we truly fall head over heels
the crazy love that would make us drop our dreams
to hear from the way his eyes look at us and say
"you're perfect"

life is a paradox

life is a paradox
beautiful yet meaningless
each breath leading to simply more inhales
each step flowing to new trails
endless beaches and dry wastelands to explore
yet nothing is ever truly sure
you could lose it all in an instant
or gain the world in a moment
floating dreaming crushing hoping
hoping vainly might i add
that the end of life will make you glad
that accomplishing meaningless goals
set by meaningless morals
will fulfill life's quotas
but my dear
they say the end is near
so enjoy life while you're here
but remember life Himself
the one thing you really need to fear

for my soul sister

the way her heart thinks
it's like a body of its own
forming words
creating unique tempos
how rare to find hearts like those
completely beautiful
and absurdly unaware of it
so common to find this oddly charming characteristic
an underground singer
a lover of the Lord
a fighter from her hearts body to the outer edges of her earthly
core
i'll dub her mystery woman, let me tell you more
she has bright eyes that have seen too much
consequently a giver
perhaps giving too much
completely wonderful
and absurdly unaware of it
she's full of many uncommon characteristics
audacious and accomplished
a woman to envy
always unassuming and lively
she would never be petty
pretty yes
kind always
she'll embrace every part of you
all of your ways
she hides her inner woman from the ones not worth the ex-
planation
but if you're lucky enough to be her chosen
what you'll discover will be truly splendid
mysterious and always unexpected

goosebumps

tense car rides
a cold breeze
they come from the same moment that makes you weak in the
knees
a new opportunity how wonderful
he might kiss me i'm beautiful
goosebumps on my body each one like a story
as if these moments bring up so many emotions within me
they burst out like a symphony
yes it's like my body is singing a silent melody trying to tell you
how this moment truly makes me feel
each little bump is an adjective that i can't bring to mind now
as my heart shudders with chills

again

here we are
we both wish it were different
i sip coffee alone and imagine you across from me
you're out with your friends feeling lonely
i deleted the songs
you still haven't changed the name of our playlists
you cook alone
and pretend to like it
hobbies aren't the same
neither is saying your name
i'd like young love to be easy
you still see right through me
i tell you it won't work
you know there's something missing
behind my eyes my mind is screaming
"won't you beg me to stay"
you purse your lips and look away
i like hard conversations
you just want to be happy
i don't want to stay here
you want to come with me
i doubt everything
your frustration begs me to trust you
i just wish you would say it so i wouldn't have to go without you
i replay all the betrayal before
you can't imagine what it's like
i want to forget and move forward
but you are just too behind
i'm running and your learning to crawl
is it worth waiting
worth the pain of a fall
i look at you and look away
you never could spit out the word
stay

the moon was big tonight
orange and low
i watched it as you held me
and stars formed above
the night sky bursting
with vibrance and life
your arm around me
changing my opinion of night
they used to be scary
the darkness consuming
now i'm in love with its stillness
this is what you do to me
i would gladly fly
to that moon in the sky
and come back to you

so that in case you didn't know
i could prove my love to you

i'd bring you back a piece of night
so we could forever remember
this time in our lives

trying to fall asleep

i wish i could hold my heart
cuddle it
wrap it in a warm blanket
and tell it everything will be okay
i hear it cry to me
but i can do nothing
i whisper to it softly
trying to comfort
its range of emotions
i wish i could hold my heart
i wish i could give it ice cream
but since i can't
i'll take deep breaths
and try try try
not to think about it

i try desperately
to remove the things
around me
that remind me of you
the problem is
you've infiltrated my very breath

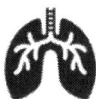

God given hair

her hair is wild as her zeal
every curl is like an intentional word
a truth spiral wrapping around the person she is loving on
giving them shelter
and love
her hair is black
but pure from the ends to the roots
she can wear darkness so boldly
because she has authority over the darkness
power and beauty
rattle with every step she takes
and with every strand that falls to the ground
she comes one step closer to wisdom
one smile closer to heaven

heartbeat

sometimes my mind wanders
and i think about your heartbeat
how it speeds up when you're scared
and slows extremely
when you sleep
how beautiful a thing it is
your heart
i long to lay my head
on your warm chest again
and melt into the comfort
your natural rhythm brings me

the idea came and went

poetry is second nature for me
but when i'm before you
i forget everything
how to write
and think
and speak
you take the breath
and the words right out of me
and i try
i try to write down these emotions you create in me
but they become like butterflies
skittish and fearful, they run from my presence
and i end up never writing a poem
face to face with you
i'm only left breathless
wordless
wonderstruck
and impressed

walking past you
pretending like i didn't see you
pretending like i never knew you
is the hardest thing
i've ever had to do

though it looks like i've moved on

i steal the words off your tongue
i take your catch phrases and use them as my own
i make our inside jokes public
i laugh and roll my eyes when someone says your name
but don't mistake this for moving on
i can't help that when i speak
the only things i can think to say are the witty comments we
used to pass back and forth
you embedded yourself into my vocabulary
and all the nick names you used to call me i have to use on other
people
not because i've moved on
but because if i don't
and i hear them later on
you will be the only face attached to the
heart shattering words
and i'll crumble
and i cannot let myself crumble
so i pretend it doesn't break my heart when someone calls me
something you used to
i act like i'm un-phased when i hear your name
but trust me
i haven't moved on

one day it makes your heart concave
then some day
you think about it
take a deep breath
and know you'll be okay

i beg the days
that i spend without you
to end
the moment the sunrises
i long for it to fall
because there's no point to a day without you
no point at all

distance and your distant disposition

there's distance between us
but i never thought you'd grow distant
i thought if we could endure the miles
we could handle life's trials
but you haven't been talking to me
just compliments and dry intimacy
what's happening
there is distance between us
but i never thought you'd grow distant so easily
i guess it's who you are
you pull away quickly
trying to protect yourself from hurting
but i'm yearning for your heart
love should never be begging
and it shouldn't tear you apart
i'm only asking that you not be so distant
i thought i knew you
but i guess i didn't

a day with friends in kona

laughter fills the car and floods out the windows
drowning in bliss
we go on adventures
to new places with the same faces
but it's never boring where joy abounds
taking pictures yet embracing
pursuing God together always chasing
after his heart, we're all racing
running our races together to get the prize
God took the blue from the sky
and put it in her eyes
he put humor of his human nature
and placed it between her smile
he put wisdom in the mind of a man
and unspeakable beauty in the body of a confident woman
likely friends and permanent siblings
bound as Christ's bride with our spiritual wedding rings
we're loved and we give love
it affects the road we drive on
and the chairs we share the gospel from
eating good meals over good talks
and taking unnaturally long walks
my gems
my friends
i want to do life with them
serving God,
seeking travel for the sake of our mission
to make disciples
and bring this love to every nation

take me down the abyss
where dreams light up the darkness
pull me down until i no longer fear falling
i'll learn falling is what brings bliss
when i say i'm scared
remind me that i wanted to be fearless
take me down the abyss
i want to see beauty
be surrounded by smiling people and not feel envy
i'll jump with you if you just promise me
the bottom of the abyss is where i can be happy
promise promise promise
and when we crash to the bottom
when we land with broken bones
and a smile
i'll believe you

HEAVENLY
MAGNOLIAS

december 20 // 2017

my hands dig into the ground
my face pushes against the floor
i can't get low enough
to come humbly before you Lord

on my knees
until they bleed
i will praise
the only one who can comfort me

my heart
and soul
and breath
and hope
and joy
my entire being rests in the fact
that you love endlessly
and that truth is a reminder needed every day

to anyone whose struggled with an eating disorder

every day is a struggle i know
i'm not going to sugar coat
it's hard to grow
but caving in is never worth it
giving up will only make you feel worthless
so i know it's hard
i know you don't want to fight anymore
i've been there before
but if you listen
you will hear it
do you hear Him
open the door
Jesus is waiting
he will heal you
it's a struggle i know
remember that he knows
he suffered like us
and he's knocking now
let him in now
let him make you new now

how abundant

grace is there in every moment of prayer
every moment of repentance during my wandering
mercy rests upon me
grace and peace
are mine in abundance
what wonderful things you give to me
i don't deserve to be sheltered under your mighty wings
but when i'm being attacked you always rescue me
you hide me
you hold me
and remind me why i love you
and how abundant are the good things that you give to those
who love you

p s a l m 3 1 :1 9

that's the beauty

you come
even when i don't know
who i am
i've lost all hope
you hold
me in your hand
and you make me new again

when i feel i'm sinking under
i'm drowning in my sin
mistakes are crushing my shoulders
i can't bear this burden
i look to you
the God of heaven
whispering to me
you remind my heart
that i will never be worthy
but that's the beauty

i've fallen short
so many times
my sincerest apologizes begin to feel like lies
i don't know who i am anymore
i've lost my faith
hope feels gone
i'm hiding from your face

that's when you remind me
of endless grace

the moment i hit my knees
the tears cease
and i sit in peace
remembering that God always fights for me

i'm so unworthy
to know you
chills overwhelm my body
at the thought of you
your presence like a lamp
your word like an iron ring
unbreakable
forever i want you to dwell in me
because without you i'm nobody
death should've been my destiny
chains could've held me in misery
but my God
you
have a hold on me
and your love will never let me go
i may never know the extent of my sin
i only know it deserves punishment but you give mercy instead
you bless me instead
and you put your right hand under my chin
you lift up my head
incline my heart to you
remind my soul about you
your promise like a rock
your peace like a river
calm and flowing forever
mercy new each day is the foundation of my faith
every day i falter
sometimes for weeks i wander
but you and your unwavering character
will still call me daughter

speak for your servant is listening

the darkness was enticing
easy to slip
i fell in but you caught me

let my words not be empty
but said with conviction toward the almighty
lift up your servant
for i am weak
i will be listening
it is you alone i seek

the world's images are senseless
the idols they create are meaningless
the world tells me i am worthless
but you call me chosen
predestined
your voice is the voice that i will always tune in

ribbon from heaven

like a colorful ribbon
you surround your people
intertwining our hearts
with your deep desires
burning within us like orange
& blue flames

your word is intricate
as complex as you are
in its fullness
my small mind feels far
your wisdom surpasses me always
and even if i meditate all my days
i won't be able to change my sinful ways
grace and incense cover the seven bowls of your wrath
i beg to see you but if you ever crossed my path
my knees would give way
my shame would burn me alive
so today
i don't ask for things with empty words
i'm asking that you bring my mind higher
you give me wisdom that goes deeper
because your intricate word is an ocean
constantly in motion
the Holy Spirit works to bring us revelations
so reveal to me
my heart is ready
my spirit is willing
give my flesh strength
give me wisdom and faith

a lifetime of poems

i'll gladly sell everything
to know your heart
if a lifetime is what you require
i lay it down from the start
love is hard work
but with you it's effortless
my life is but a breath
and i want to spend it in your presence
you buy me white dresses
and carry my burdens
i will rest in your caresses
i will wait on my love
i will sing for you and dance
you're the only one in my audience
from the stage i caught your glance
i'm now forever in a willing trance
the pursuit of knowing you
is my life's only calling
for others to feel this loved
is my only longing
i love you i love you
with all that i am
with my thoughts and my pen
i'll bring you a lifetime of poems
you have eyes only for me
yet everyone together is your bride to be
like a flower you plant me
and water my seeds
i'll grow into a tree
you'll make my leaves bright green
and you promise me eternity
forever i'll be with you
this is my greatest treat
i'll bring you poems from down here
and in heaven i'll kiss your feet

you're our only love

come like the sun

consume us oh Son

i can't sleep
i can't sleep without your peace
wash afresh over me
let's turn over a new leaf
let's start over
i'll work harder
at honest surrender
if you meet me again
i can't know how it ends
but i know how i'll begin
smashing all that i own
at your feet
at your throne
you're the one in the heavenly seat
i'm just living to make you known

ecclesia

a city on a hill
a lamp on a stand
we seek the Lord's will
we're guided by his hand
no force of hell
could ever stand
against the love
of our King for His people
we don't worship him
for fame or glory
but honor his name
with every story
his mighty word and the blood of our testimony
this is our mission
pointing the world toward he who is holy
it's time to rise
and take back what's His
the fire in his eyes
is passion for his children
our feet have been anointed
our hands have been called
we have no other option
but to follow his heart
his heart is for the lost
the rejected and poor
we'll go at any cost
because we want more
together is how we go
because without each other
we'll never know
the full extension of his halo
there's fire in our words
and peace in our hearts
because we know who we worship
he's known the end from the start
we cannot be hidden

our light can't be dimmed
we broke off our sin
now there's a brighter spirit within

a dinner with Jesus

what do you think about yellow
does it mean happiness to you
how high does the sky go
is it your favorite blue
what do you think about pasta
marinara or pesto
do you like making jokes
and when you're sick
will you drink a coke
i see many different aspects of your personality

what do you think of me
do you love me even when i hurt you
did you ever feel unseen
lost in a crowd who don't know what's true
how did it feel when your people deserted you
how can you be so full of mercy
your kindness overwhelms me
can i know you more
will you knock on my door
i'm begging you to dine with me
sit and do life with me
because i have many more questions
about the ocean and trees
will you be my portion
and never let go of me

you are the God
who brings honey from rocks
lighting from clear skies
and water to dry land
you're the same God
from beginning to end
by your first breath
galaxies are still being formed
you're worthy of my life
so i will not be conformed
my God is the same God
who raised the dead to life
my God rescued me from the darkest of nights
there's nothing above him
he's always been good
and my God
is the father
who cares for the misunderstood
let the nations repent
for not listening to his voice
let the nations turn
for he's coming to destroy
now is the time of salvation
it won't be this way forever
so give back what is the Fathers
and lay your life down in surrender
this life is but a vapor
his kingdom endures forever

p s a l m 8 1 : 1 6

you purify me
and give me eyes to see
my destiny
matters more to you than to me
my focus is not this earth
but on your surpassing worth

occupied

what gain could i make
that compares to your grace
what knowledge could i find
to be greater than your time
i trust your control and give up mine
what little i can do here
i will do for you my dear
you occupy my hours
but i'm begging you
take every minute
i'm not satisfied with life
but sitting in your presence i find it
it being wisdom
wisdom that reveals to me
just how little my efforts really mean
you occupy my time
and every thought that crosses my mind
you wrap in joy
and tie them up in a bow of peace
let my worship to you
never cease
there's nothing else for me
i can finally see
you were always waiting to supply my every need
and i being a fool
thought i had to work to receive
but you keep me occupied with joy in my heart
the good things i have here are only the start
the bad things that come my way
will be made into art
i'll see the fruit of all these things one day
but for now i'm busy
gazing into your eyes
laughing because *lovesickness makes me dizzy*

e c c l e s i a s t e s 5 : 2 0

the word

if i know your heart more
i'll understand your word more
you gave us this gift
full access to knowing you
but it's just complex enough
that we still have to ask you
for wisdom and such things
you want a relationship with us it seems
you're wonderfully complex yet so lovingly relatable
you understand our suffering but you still flip our tables
you love us too much to let us do it wrong
but you're patient with us as we seek to know you more

let your word come alive
as paragraphs turn into flowers
forming a garden of explanation
opening our minds to the story of creation

i'm begging you to knock me off the throne
the space i made for you to dwell
somehow became my own
and i don't like it this way
i want you to hold the reigns
you have always been and will always be first place
who am i to argue about sitting at your right hand
your wonderful throne of grace
too perfect for me to comprehend
knock me off of the throne
because
you're the one who loved me first
you are the lover of a prostitute bride
you still see the light in my eyes
when i cry
though i'm ashamed of the way i took your place

my heart weeps at the thought of receiving grace

i beg you
cast me away
it's what i deserve
you love a prostitute bride
who dishonors your word
i break my heart when i hurt you
i can't imagine what you feel
love still sees me pure
and i know this love is real

i'm low as can be
begging for a fresh understanding of mercy
your truth is the only one i want to hear ringing
quiet my mind of my own thoughts
let me hear what you're saying
what you're repeating

i s a i a h 2 8 : 1 0

"who can enter the kingdom of heaven"

"by grace through faith"

take me for example
a mess more often than not
confused and quick to anger
slow to bring my cares to the Lord
my shoes are fit for sharing the gospel
but my own fear unties them most days
sometimes i live in a daze
apathetic to God
the one who gives me each breath to begin with
i forget what matters
and dive headfirst into shallow promises i knew
would never go deeper
i give up on myself
i get mad and sad
and i sin
i sin against the one i love more than life itself
i hurt him and i hurt me and the cycle becomes like a movie
where the soon bride to be
paces up and down the aisle unsure if he's actually worth while
though i am unworthy to be called loved by the King
i made my vow
and he sealed it with a ring
the end result is not a mystery
the deleted scenes show us happy
but it was
not when i finally got myself together
only when I dove headfirst into the promise of grace
which i should've known
would always go deeper

i want to gaze at your eyes
like it's the very first time

keep walking

in a span of fifty feet
i hear a couple fighting as the husband shouts for a divorce
and swears to end their lifelong promise
after just thirteen short years
i see a little boy sheepishly say hi to me from the other side of
the road
and i smile and wave
then i cry
and ask God why
is the world so broken
how could i see such heart sinking destruction
and walk on to see such a beautiful portrait that is youth
the things that make life worth living
are next door to the brokenness of hearts unbinding
his answer to me was keep walking

you captured me once and forever

it gets me every time
if you don't know
it's a lot like a really warm hug
from someone you love
every time i enter His presence
well
not every time
 but even if it's only tonight
it's enough

surrendered to your love

i love you a lot
 but we all know who loves who more

engraved

it stings like a nail
rubbing along the skin
it aches like a broken heart
when you lose a close friend
it feels so heavy
like carrying the weight of the world
each letter of your name
felt like a whip digging into my skin
but the whole time
i was thinking it was worth it
it burns like sour wine
going into the depths of an empty stomach
it haunts like a nightmare
thinking about the ones i can't save
my heart breaks like a glass vase
seeing my children go astray
it kills
as if my child was ripped from my womb
it's dark like the world's remedies
without the Son the sun loses its energy
it hurts
it hurts like getting slapped
when you try to give a gift
it could've been an eternal rift
but i engraved your name onto my body
with every hit and whip
nobody said sorry
but it was so worth it
your name looks so beautiful on me
perfectly permanently with me
for a moment it ached
but now there can be harmony

hearing the gospel

just like trying new food
you won't ever know you're lacking something
until someone introduces it to you

follow the leader

you are the pilot
and the captain
my leader
first in command
you are the most righteous
you are the most humble
you are in full control
you are judge
defender
lover
merciful giver
you are a sacrifice
my king
you are all i need
you are teacher
Father
perfect role model
Lord
and human
you are
the driver
and you paved the road
you are God
Adonai
Jehovah
you are jealous for me
since that is all true
i will gladly follow you

God?

and you feel like a wisp
a forethought
just a wallpaper
not moving
i don't feel you
i know *i can* see you
 but most of the time
i skim right over you

be still

perfectly still
yet fully in motion
how the earth moves
& how you wish for us to live

morning

and i say good morning to you
with a smile
because time doesn't hold you
and this makes the morning even more special

you gifted us a chance to catch stillness before our days' work
begins
and i will forever smile about it

loving God

i'm learning how to have a relationship with you
learning that some days i don't feel like doing what we always
do
today
i just want to sit here
you can read to me
and i'll tell you what i'm thinking
we should be more spontaneous
more wild you and me
this was never just fun
you're my everything
and i want to hear about what's on your heart
and make you happy
because i'm learning everyday
how to love you

aubade

you command me to look at your greatness
& i see
you control the birds
the sky lights up pink because you like colorful things
the ocean
too massive
too deep
to hold your love
i put my camera down
and i see it now
i see you'll never fail me
and that your grace is as simply complex as the sea

peace

one second of connection with you
is enough
calmness
surpassing the feeling after an *hour* of meditation

me and you and the sky

grace surrounds me like a blanket of stars
when i feel like i'm in an endless black hole

Made in the USA
Columbia, SC
03 March 2021